WHAT IS THE
UNPARDONABLE
SIN?

Doug Batchelor

Roseville, CA

Published by
Amazing Facts International
P. O. Box 1058
Roseville, CA 95678-8058
800-538-7275
www.afbookstore.com

Special recognition to Joe Crews for some shared content
from his book *The Point of No Return*. Copyright © 2006
by Lu Ann Crews. Published by Amazing Facts, Inc.

Cover design by Haley Trimmer
Text design by Greg Solie • AltamontGraphics.com

ISBN 978-1-58019-508-9

WHAT IS THE
UNPARDONABLE
SIN?

A man visiting Scotland for the first time went to a place on the coast featuring a beautiful bay beach. Up along the beach, soft, sandy hills rose up sharply into a steep, rocky cliff that dropped down right along the narrow shore. The man was enjoying his time, meditating and studying the shells. He noticed the tide had gone out, exposing a lot of new beautiful rocks and shells. So he continued to walk—the ocean on one side, the beach beneath him, and the sheer rock cliff wall that stretched for miles on the other side.

As he traveled up the shore, he came to a rusted steel post in the ground hoisting a metal sign that had words painted in bold, clear letters:

"Warning!
Danger: If you go beyond this point, you will not be able to escape the incoming tide."

The man looked behind him and thought, "*Well, I might not be a marathon runner, but I can surely get back to the safe zone before the tide overtakes me. I'd like to go a little farther. These are some of the best shells and tidal pools I've ever seen.*" Besides, the tide was a good way off.

He walked on, well past the sign—preoccupied with the starfish, seashells, and curious little crabs that were now skittering from hole to hole. Along the way, every so often, he would think: *I'll just keep an eye on the surf and, when I see it start to change, I'll head back to the safe section of the beach.*

But once he had gone beyond that sign, he had already gone too far. He did not realize in that part of Scotland, during certain seasons and moon phases, the tidal cycle is often powerful and swift. So he kept walking, meandering along the wet sand.

Not long after, he saw the tide had changed and the waves were beginning to come in, so he turned around. But the tide was surging very fast, charging in like a galloping horse. He'd never seen a tide roll in so quickly! No sooner had he turned to make a hasty retreat, than the waves were upon him like miniature tsunamis. He began to run, but the rising waves slapped against his legs, repeatedly knocking him over. Soon the waves were dragging him right up against the rocky cliffs!

People sightseeing above the cliffs saw him struggling and watched helplessly as the man was pummeled time and time again against the unforgiving sheer rock.

His lifeless body was found the next day.

What happened? He had gone beyond the warning sign.

Yes—he was alive and well for a while after he passed the warning sign, but there actually was no hope because he had reached the point of no return.

There is, in certain situations, a very clear point of no return. The military even has a term for it: "PNR."

And with good reason too. We hear about Navy helicopters that are sent on rescue missions. As they're flying out over the ocean from their aircraft carrier, they have a special instrument labeled PNR*—the point of no return. When they reach a certain point, an alarm goes off. It tells them, basically, that it's now or never—they've reached the halfway point of their fuel supply. It means that, even if they see the person they're trying to rescue just a little farther beyond, if they continue to fly away from their vessel, as well-intentioned as they might be, based on the laws of physics, they are going to run out of fuel before they can get back. They'll be ditching in the ocean.

Like that man who died on the Scottish shore, if they don't turn around right then and there, they might not make it home by air.

No Turning Back?

Along these same lines, the Bible teaches that there is a point you can go to in sinning against God where your life might still be active—your lungs are breathing, your heart is beating—but you are doomed, just as surely as if the gates of Hades had already closed behind you. That is, it is possible for a person to have gone so far away from God, from the promptings of the Holy Spirit, that they have spiritually reached the point of no return and, perhaps, even have gone well past it.

It is called the "unpardonable sin," and we're dealing with this because so many worried and confused

---

* Now also called "Point of Equal Time" (PET) or "Critical Point" (CP).

Christians are wondering, "Have I committed the unpardonable sin? What hope can you give me?"

No question, in our ministry, we frequently meet those who have wondered if they have committed this unforgivable sin. A man feels his prayers seem to bounce back from the ceiling, or a woman feels there is no hope of receiving God's favor or forgiveness. Yet they can't identify any particular sinful act that severed them from the hope of salvation. God just seems silent. How can they tell if they have actually committed the unpardonable sin? Can any person really know?

Why Does This Matter?

A few years ago the psychology department of Duke University carried on an interesting experiment. (It would never be allowed today.) They wanted to see how long rats could swim based on hope. In one container surrounded by sheer walls, they placed a rat for whom there was no possibility of escape. He swam in circles a few moments and then gave up, resigned to drown. In the other container, they made the hope of escape possible for the rat. A little ladder was placed just out of reach. The rat swam for several hours before finally drowning. We usually say, "As long as there is life, there is hope." The Duke experiment proved, "As long as there is hope, there is life."

Some people believe they have committed the unforgivable sin and have lost hope and stopped living.

So before answering these troubling questions about the unpardonable sin, a glorious truth first needs to be recognized: We serve a God of infinite love and compassion! It is not His will that anyone be lost. He has made provision in His Word for every soul to be forgiven and saved. The incredible promise of 1 John 1:9 applies to every man, woman, and child in the world today: "If we confess our sins, he is faithful and just to forgive us our sins, and to cleanse us from all unrighteousness."

On the condition of a sincere confession, God promises to forgive any sin, regardless of its nature.

> "Come now, and let us reason together," says the LORD, "Though your sins are like scarlet, they shall be as white as snow; though they are red like crimson, they shall be as wool" (Isaiah 1:18).

Here God is saying, "*You have sinned. I know that. But I still love you and want you to have salvation so badly that I sent my Son to die on the cross for you, to pay the penalty for your sins. Why, therefore, don't you accept what I have done for you?*"

What a special assurance for those who have violated every law of God and man in their wild plunge into degradation. God loves them still! There is no guilt too great for Him to cleanse away. He waits with outstretched arms to receive those who take the first step toward His forgiveness and mercy. After all, look at what happened at the cross! The ultimate price was paid for our redemption from sin. The God who would do that for us wants us to have the salvation He offers, a salvation that cost Him so much.

At the same time, however, people can commit the unpardonable sin, which will put them out of the reach of salvation and eternal life. What is this sin which heaven regards with such abhorrence? Why, too, will God deal so severely with those who are guilty of it?

To the human mind, a great number of depraved and cruel acts might fall into such a category, but which one of them would God count so heinous that it could never be forgiven? This is the crucial question that we are going to explore in this short book.

A Fearsome Warning

Let's first look at what the Bible specifically says about this sin.

Indeed, the most fearful words ever spoken by Jesus had to do with the fateful possibility of committing the unpardonable sin. He said,

> "Therefore I say to you, every sin and blasphemy will be forgiven men, but the blasphemy against the Spirit will not be forgiven men" (Matthew 12:31).

Here it is again:

> "Assuredly, I say to you, all sins will be forgiven the sons of men, and whatever blasphemies they may utter; but he who blasphemes against the Holy Spirit never has forgiveness, but is subject to eternal condemnation" (Mark 3:28, 29).

And again, in Luke 12:10:

"And anyone who speaks a word against the Son of Man, it will be forgiven him; but to him who blasphemes against the Holy Spirit, it will not be forgiven."

Let's look at these texts closely. "I say to you," Jesus said, "every sin and blasphemy will be forgiven." We should be so thankful that the Lord is a God who forgives "every sin and blasphemy." After all, human beings are capable of some pretty gruesome and depraved acts, are we not? And yet Jesus here is very clear: *All can be forgiven.* That's how powerful and effectual Christ's death on the cross was. It was enough to cover every sin and blasphemy.

But we would be remiss to end right here, because Jesus doesn't end right here.

He goes on to say something very grave. He says that the "blasphemy against the Spirit *will not be* forgiven men." Amazing! "Anyone who speaks a word against the Son of Man, it will be forgiven him." Yet blasphemy against the Holy Spirit will *not* be forgiven!

Right after some religious leaders in Israel, in cahoots with the Romans, crucified Jesus, He prayed, "Father, forgive them." Would Jesus have uttered that prayer if it was not possible for them to be forgiven? Even something as horrible as crucifying the Son of God was forgivable.

But what did Jesus say in another place? "But whoever speaks against the Holy Spirit, it will not be forgiven him, either in this age or in the age to come" (Matthew 12:32).

That's heavy! They could be forgiven for driving nails into Jesus' hands and hoisting him up on a ragged cross but not for "speaking" against the Holy Spirit. No forgiveness—not now, not in judgment day, not in the resurrection ... *not ever!*

Again, we see this same contrast in Mark: "All sins will be forgiven the sons of men, and whatever blasphemies they may utter." That's encouraging; is it not? God is so merciful that He can forgive us *all* sins and blasphemy. But then we are given this warning: "But he who blasphemes against the Holy Spirit never has forgiveness, but is subject to eternal condemnation" (Mark 3:28, 29).

How much clearer could Jesus be? We obviously don't want to blaspheme against the Holy Spirit because it will lead to "eternal condemnation." Thus, how important it is that we learn two things:

- First, what does it mean to "utter blasphemy" against the Holy Spirit?

- Second, how can we make sure that we don't do it?

What the Unpardonable Sin Is Not

Now, whenever people hear about the unpardonable sin, their first question is, *"What is it?"*

In search of the answer, they often go the book of Exodus and look through the Ten Commandments, where they try to conjure up what they think is the worst possible sin; that sin is surely, they surmise, the unpardonable one.

For instance, one might believe that innocent life is certainly the most important thing, and if someone were to take an innocent life—that is, commit murder—that would have to be the unpardonable sin.

After all, once a person is dead, there's nothing that can be done to bring that person back.

That makes sense, of course. Murder is horrendous. However, we clearly find examples in the Bible of those guilty of murder who we believe will be in heaven.

First, there's Moses. Exodus 2:12 says the great prophet "looked this way and that way, and when he saw no one, he killed the Egyptian and hid him in the sand." That was the sin of murder. God didn't want Moses to commit it, but God did forgive the imperfect prophet and even used Moses to do a great work in leading the children of Israel out of Egypt.

How about David? In 2 Samuel 12:9, the prophet Nathan said to David, "Why have you despised the commandment of the LORD, to do evil in His sight? You have killed Uriah the Hittite with the sword; you have taken his wife to be your wife, and have killed him with the sword of the people of Ammon." So, besides murder, we can add adultery to David's grievous sin. Neither murder nor adultery, bad as they are (and they are bad), can be the unpardonable sin, because we know from the Bible that God forgave David both of these sins—though, of course, the king did have to live with the terrible consequences of his sins, which is another matter entirely.

In our culture, perhaps the worst crime is when someone sexually abuses or otherwise harms or kills an innocent child. Truly, how much lower can a person stoop? Even Jesus says, "Whoever causes one of these little ones who believe in Me to stumble, it would be better for him if a millstone were hung around his neck, and he were thrown into the sea" (Mark 9:42).

If anything were the unpardonable sin, one would think it would be harming an innocent child.

This crime is actually mentioned in the Bible too. As a matter of fact, in some pagan nations, infanticide was part of their worship. They would kill their children and burn them on altars, all to supposedly appease their gods. In the Bible, it's referred to as making their children "pass through the fire."

It's referenced in Ezekiel 16:20–22 as one of the things that was especially offensive to the Lord regarding the nations that surrounded Israel. But what made matters worse was that some Israelites began doing the same thing to *their own children.* Despite all the light that they had been given, they had fallen into one of the most awful and degrading of all pagan practices! "They even sacrificed their sons and their daughters to demons" (Psalm 106:37). Now what could be worse than that—especially for a people who should have known better because of all the special revelations given to them as God's chosen nation?

But there's somebody in the Bible who did this, yet, according to the biblical record, we can believe that person is forgiven. Manasseh was a king in Israel who was guilty of infanticide. A king! 2 Kings 21:6 says: "He made his son pass through the fire, practiced soothsaying, used witchcraft, and consulted spiritists and mediums. He did much evil in the sight of the LORD, to provoke Him to anger." It was child sacrifice, pure and simple. But you read on and the Bible tells us that this king fully repented, accepted the Lord, and even implemented a reformation in Israel.

It's unimaginable to us that someone, after they get involved in child sacrifice, could be forgiven. God is, obviously, more gracious and merciful than most of us would be, that's for sure!

(Maybe you've heard of Ted Bundy, a vicious serial killer of young women. The murders were especially horrific. When he was finally caught and put in prison on death row, he confessed and ostensibly went through a conversion process and accepted Jesus. The respected family counselor Dr. James Dobson went to visit Bundy before his execution, and the Christian leader came away believing that God can even forgive someone who did the horrible things that Bundy did, as unimaginable as that might seem to us.)

Thus, when Jesus says there's a sin for which you can't be forgiven, it must be really bad! Worse than adultery... worse than murder... even worse than child sacrifice!

Could it be the act of denying Christ? Well, can we think of somebody in the Bible who openly and blatantly denied Christ yet was forgiven? The book of Matthew records how Peter swore up and down that he would be faithful to Jesus no matter what. However, when accused of being a follower of Christ, he openly denied it—three times, even! "Then he began to curse and to swear." It was bad enough that he denied Christ, but he did it with cursing and swearing as well! (See Matthew 26:69–75.)

Publicly denying Christ, renouncing that you know Him, and doing it with an oath and foul language... that's pretty bad, especially for someone who had been as privileged as Peter, who had been part of Jesus' intimate inner circle for so long and who had seen so many miracles! Could that sin be forgiven?

Obviously it can, because Peter was not only forgiven his sin, he also became a leader in the early New Testament church. Here are the words of Jesus to him after Jesus had been raised from the dead:

> "So when they had eaten breakfast, Jesus said to Simon Peter, 'Simon, son of Jonah, do you love Me more than these?' He said to Him, 'Yes, Lord; You know that I love You.' He said to him, 'Feed My lambs.' He said to him again a second time, 'Simon, son of Jonah, do you love Me?' He said to Him, 'Yes, Lord; You know that I love You.' He said to him, 'Tend My sheep.' He said to him the third time, 'Simon, son of Jonah, do you love Me?' Peter was grieved because He said to him the third time, 'Do you love Me?' And he said to Him, 'Lord, You know all things; You know that I love You.' Jesus said to him, 'Feed My sheep'" (John 21:15–17).

If that doesn't sound like forgiveness, what does?

What About Suicide?

This is obviously a very emotionally charged subject. Indeed, who doesn't know, either directly or indirectly, someone who committed suicide? Sometimes suicidal people call our radio program asking, "If I commit suicide, can I still be saved?" What do you think we tell them? We discourage them in every way possible. We suggest to them that if the last act of a person's life is an act of utter hopelessness and faith-lessness, and if the Bible tells us that without faith it's impossible to please God, what can we say? We do all we can to dissuade them from the thought, reminding them if the last act of their lives is self-murder, obvious-ly, that wouldn't bode very well for their eternal future.

At the same time, who doesn't know someone whose loved one, a child, perhaps, has taken his or her own life? These dear people are so devastated by the thought that a loved one's next conscious thought is that they are eternally lost, they do everything they can in their reasoning to widen that gate. And, indeed, we need to be careful not to be dogmatic about the eternal destiny of anyone, including a suicide. Only God knows the state of the heart and mind in those last moments of life.

Besides, we have an example in the Bible of some-one who committed suicide yet was still deemed faith-ful: Samson. Judges 16:30 reads, "Then Samson said, 'Let me die with the Philistines!' And he pushed with all his might, and the temple fell." Yes, the temple fell on the lords of the Philistines, killing them, but its walls also fell on Samson. Some might argue, "*Look, they were getting ready to kill him anyway; he just thought to take his enemy with him. Thus, Samson's act of war was re-ally a sacrifice and not a suicide.* Nevertheless, Samson knew that by knocking down the walls, he would kill himself as well—and that is a form of suicide.

Will Samson be in heaven? In Hebrews 11, he's listed among the faithful. Suicide, though tragic in ev-ery way, cannot be the unpardonable sin.

The Horror of Hopelessness

On December 17, 1927, while surfacing, the US-S-4 submarine was accidentally rammed and sunk by the Coast Guard destroyer *Paulding*. The entire crew was trapped in its prison house of death. Ships rushed to the scene of disaster off the coast of Massachusetts, where the doomed men clung to life as the oxygen slowly gave out.

A diver placed his helmeted ear to the side of the vessel and listened. He heard a tapping noise. Someone was tapping out a question in the dots and dashes of Morse code. The question came slowly: "Is … there … any … hope?"

Sadly, despite their best efforts, there was no reason for hope and all six men perished.

This seems to be the cry of humanity: "Is there any hope?" Hope, indeed, is the basis of all human existence in Christ!

You have heard the expression, "Where there is life there is hope." This comes from the Bible, where Solomon says, "But for him who is joined to all the living there is hope, for a living dog is better than a dead lion" (Ecclesiastes 9:4).

So far we have looked at some pretty heavy sins, and yet we have reason to believe that, as bad as these sins are, not one of them is the unpardonable sin that Jesus spoke so strongly about.

What, then, is the sin that is so bad that it cannot be forgiven, no matter what? What sin is so bad that even the death of Jesus isn't enough to save the guilty one from condemnation? What sin leaves them with no hope?

After all these years, who isn't still disturbed by the images from the 9/11 attacks on America? Some are very graphic, like when photographers captured images of those desperate and trapped workers in the World Trade Center. They have photos of people on the higher floors who found their way to the windows in an effort to escape the flames. They couldn't make it down because the fires trapped them, but once they got to the windows, then what? In some cases, they were 40 stories above the ground, yet with no other recourse, they jumped to their deaths rather than be burned alive inside the building. Talk about utter hopelessness!

Or what about this situation? He was a parachute instructor who had spent so much time making sure that his students were all suited up and cinched in tight that one day he had forgotten, believe it or not, to put on his own parachute. He then jumped out of the airplane to his death! Can you imagine what he must have felt like on the way down, knowing that he was going to die? All that training for others ... yet he ended up doing something so careless. Again, talk about an awful sense of hopelessness!

We use these two sad stories as an analogy for what it must be like to have the Lord declare to a person, a family, a nation, a city, or the world that there's no hope for them, that they are eternally lost. To still be alive and know that your situation is hopeless is a dreadful thought. It's like that with the unpardonable sin, the one sin that cannot be forgiven. So again we ask, "What is it?"

Blasphemy

As we saw above, in Luke 12:10, Jesus said, "Anyone who speaks a word against the Son of Man, it will be forgiven him; but to him who ***blasphemes*** against the Holy Spirit, it will not be forgiven" (emphasis supplied). It is someone who "blasphemes" who cannot be forgiven. Thus, we need to decipher what blasphemy is, because, obviously, it is a crucial component to understanding the unpardonable sin.

In the Greek, the word is *blasphemos* and, according to one dictionary's concise definition, it means "to vilify, to speak impiously, to defame, to rail upon, to revile, to speak evil, to hurt or blast the reputation, nature or works of God." So to speak evil of God— to defame, to vilify, to undermine Him with your words—is blasphemy. There are some other definitions, but this one is principally the one that Jesus uses in this warning.

In the *American Heritage Dictionary*, blasphemy is defined as "a contemptuous or profane act, utterance, or writing concerning God or a sacred entity." It also gives another definition: "the act of claiming for oneself the attributes and rights of God." We actually believe this last one is closer to the definition we're looking for when the Bible speaks of blasphemy against the Holy Spirit. But if you aren't sure about dictionary definitions, then let's let the Bible define itself.

In the Bible, we find some stories in which blasphemy is cited, such as in John 10:33. At one point, some of the leaders in Israel were trying to find a reason to stone Jesus. "The Jews answered Him, saying, 'For a good work we do not stone You, but for blasphemy, and because You, being a Man, make Yourself God.'" Thus, man putting himself in the place of God is a Bible definition of blasphemy, just as it was in the dictionary.

Now look at Luke 5:21. "And the scribes and the Pharisees began to reason, saying, 'Who is this who speaks blasphemies? Who can forgive sins but God alone?'" Now, Jesus had just said He could forgive the sins of a paralytic. The religious leaders were angry, because they realized that by forgiving the man's sin, Jesus was putting Himself in the place of God.

In other words, suggesting that what you think is more important than what God says. Isn't that putting yourself in the place of God? Some people might not have considered that they're at risk of committing the unpardonable sin because they are claiming the prerogatives of God for themselves. They're making themselves their own god. They're not listening to the words of God; instead, they're saying, "My reasons are more important than the commandments of God." *A man putting himself in the place of God.* That's pretty heavy. If that's not blasphemy, what is?

Of course, blasphemy itself is not the unpardonable sin. In fact, we all have probably committed varying degrees of blasphemy at some point or another. After all, the apostle Paul had been a blasphemer, and we can be assured that Paul will be in heaven. In 1 Timothy 1:13, he writes: "Although I was formerly a blasphemer, a persecutor, and an insolent man; but I obtained mercy because I did it ignorantly in unbelief."

God's grace to us is exceedingly abundant; it forgives even blasphemy. Indeed, right in Matthew 12:31,

Jesus says: "Every sin and *blasphemy* will be forgiven men" (emphasis supplied). Again, God's grace is amazing! All kinds of blasphemy are forgiven ... *except the blasphemy against the Holy Spirit.*

Thus, in order to understand what blasphemy against the Holy Spirit is, we also need to understand what the Holy Spirit does. Once we grasp that, we can then better understand what it means to blaspheme the Holy Spirit and why it's been deemed the unpardonable sin.

Three Functions

What does the Holy Spirit do? Why is His function so crucial that blasphemy against Him is so serious a sin that it cannot be forgiven?

Jesus said, "But the Helper, the Holy Spirit, whom the Father will send in My name, He will teach you all things, and bring to your remembrance all things that I said to you" (John 14:26). First, the Holy Spirit teaches us things—the things we need to know for our salvation.

Next, besides teaching us all things, Jesus indicated that the Spirit will also "guide you into all truth" (John 16:13). Every searching student of the Word has probably experienced this guiding influence of the Holy Spirit. There can be no true insight into biblical truth without the enlightenment of this Spirit of God.

Finally, the mission of the Holy Spirit is to convict of sin. Jesus said, "It is to your advantage that I go away; for if I do not go away, the Helper will not come to you; but if I depart, I will send Him to you. And when He has come, He will convict the world of sin,

20

and of righteousness, and of judgment" (John 16:7, 8). It is the special work of the Holy Spirit to reprove us and convict us of our sin. When wrongs are committed, the conscience is pricked with a sense of guilt—that is the work of the Holy Spirit.

Thus, we see that the Holy Spirit 1) teaches us what we need to know, 2) guides us into truth, and 3) convicts of sin. This is His work. It is logical, therefore, to conclude that as long as we allow the Holy Spirit to teach us, to guide us, and to convict us, we could never be guilty of committing the unpardonable sin.

But suppose we refuse to acknowledge these three operations of the Spirit in our personal experience with God? That is exactly when people begin to approach the deadly parameters of the worst sin on record.

A Powerful Example

It is intriguing to study the actual examples of the unpardonable sin in the Bible record. For instance, at one time, practically everyone in the world passed over that point of no return. Here is what the Bible says about the state of the world before the global flood: "And the LORD said, 'My Spirit *shall not strive with man forever*, for he is indeed flesh; yet his days shall be one hundred and twenty years'" (Genesis 6:3, emphasis added). That's a scary declaration!

God is saying that at some point, enough is enough. Look at what the pre-flood people were like: "Then the LORD saw that the wickedness of man was great in the earth, and that every intent of the thoughts of his heart was only evil continually. And the LORD was sorry that He had made man on the earth, and He was grieved in His heart" (Genesis 6:5, 6). If every thought of their hearts was evil, imagine what their words and deeds were like! They were so bad that God was even sorry that He had created them.

These texts speak of the antediluvian world, which perished in the global flood. For more than 100 years, the Holy Spirit pleaded with that wicked generation through the preaching of Noah. Although the imagination of nearly every heart was evil continually, a small remnant responded to the Spirit and entered the ark. All the rest were swept away in the raging waters, which covered every inch of the earth's surface. After years of patient striving, the Spirit withdrew to leave the stubborn sinners to their chosen fate.

Could the same thing happen again? There is an amazing parallel between the days of Noah and today. Jesus said, "As it was in the days of Noah, so it will be also in the days of the Son of Man" (Luke 17:26). The very same excesses of the pre-flood world are being committed right now in the great cities of our world. Perversions of the worst degree continue to mark the carnal course of every nation under the sun as few seek the safety of God's hands.

It's curious, of course. Why did the vast majority of pre-flood people refuse to enter the ark of safety? Many of them probably helped Noah construct that huge vessel; they saw all the animals go aboard peacefully. Surely the Holy Spirit stirred them with conviction, but they would not obey the message. Finally, God said, "Let them alone. My Spirit will no longer strive with them."

Here we see a key issue that should help us understand the point of no return. God's Holy Spirit no longer strove among those people. That is, they were so hardened in their rejection of the Spirit and His pleadings with them that God finally had to say enough is enough—no more.

We also see here at a corporate level what we're trying to find on an individual one: what it means to spurn the Holy Spirit at such a level that nothing more can be done for us because we have, indeed, reached the PNR—the point of no return.

How crucial, then, it is for us as individuals to make sure we don't make the same mistake that these people did and fall headlong into the same trap.

Conviction

The good news is that we don't have to fall into that trap, not as long as we cooperate with the Holy Spirit in our lives. Remember, one of the things He does is convict us of wrongdoing. "When He has come, He will convict the world of sin" (John 16:8). To refuse, to reject, and to harden yourself against the convicting influence of the Spirit cannot be something good. Indeed, as we just saw with those who lived before the flood, it's a big step toward crossing the PNR.

Think about it: Is it good to be convicted? If you are standing in a house that's caught on fire, your nerves tell you to run. But if you ignore that pain from the heat, you're going to burn. Indeed, pain can be a healthy thing if it helps you preserve your life, right? Some unfortunate people have a disease that deadens the pain nerves in their body. It might sound attractive to be unable to experience pain, but the problem is that the people with this disease sustain all sorts of injuries the rest of us don't. For instance, if we were to put our hand on a hot stove, we would instantly pull it away. They wouldn't pull away because they wouldn't feel the pain; hence, they would get badly burned in a way we would not.

Thus pain—conviction—at the right time, in the right place, is very important. And that's especially true when it comes to the work of the Holy Spirit in bringing to us the conviction of sin. It was the conviction of the Holy Spirit that led the men to ask Peter, "What shall we do [to be saved]?" (Acts 2:37). They were convicted; it was a healthy thing. Yet suppose they were so hardened against the Spirit that they ignored Peter and his powerful preaching. One of the most important questions we can ask is, "What must I do to be saved?" *If you don't ask it, if you don't care about being saved, what hope is there for you?*

Indeed, what if you had a son who was regularly given to cursing, lying, and stealing without any feelings of guilt? Would that not worry you? Wouldn't you want your kid's conscience to bother him about wrongdoing? You certainly wouldn't want your son to feel good, to boast in doing evil! You would want him to be convicted and to act upon that conviction of wrongdoing, right? It's an encouraging thing to see your child feel remorseful about doing wrong. It's a sign of growth. But if he's morally calloused and doesn't have any conviction, that's very dangerous and any parent should be concerned.

Perhaps you remember the story in the book of Exodus about the Pharaoh of Egypt. Talk about someone seeing evidence of the Spirit! What monarch saw more miracles than he did? Moses would even come and schedule out the miracles. He'd say there was going to be a divine plague the next day, and it happened. Pharaoh personally witnessed the power of God. How stubborn does one have to be to see a pillar of fire, to see the Red Sea part, to see the Jews marching through the sea, and yet be so bent on resisting the evidence of God's Spirit that he would still attack His people?

Can you imagine how nervous those Egyptian soldiers were as they saw the sea part and the children of Israel pass through it on dry ground? They could clearly see that God was with those people. "*You want us to do what? You still want us to attack them after all these plagues to deliver them?*" How stubborn and ornery can someone be? It's as if you'd have to be possessed by another spirit, a dark spirit, to be that obstinate.

Well, Pharaoh was that stubborn, and that is what destroyed him in the end—along with his entire army. He allowed his own heart to become hardened. He was not able to acknowledge that he was wrong. Despite all the incredible miracles he had seen, despite all the evidence that he had witnessed, even the death of his own first-born son, he refused to acknowledge the power and sovereignty of the living God.

Take a moment to read these powerful words from the writer E. G. White:

"God had declared concerning Pharaoh, 'I will harden his heart, that he shall not let the people go' (Exodus 4:21). There was no exercise of supernatural power to harden the heart of the king. God gave to Pharaoh the most striking evidence of divine power, but the monarch stubbornly refused to heed the light. Every display of infinite power rejected by him, rendered him the more determined in his rebellion. The seeds of rebellion that he sowed when he rejected the first miracle produced their harvest. As he continued to venture on in his own course, going from one degree of stubbornness to another, his heart became more and more hardened, until he was called to look upon the cold, dead faces of the first-born" (*Patriarchs and Prophets*, p. 261).

We're now seeing more clearly what this blasphemy against the Holy Spirit involves. We should also start to discern that this lethal sin isn't just one horrible isolated deed, but a constant rejection of the work that the Holy Spirit is seeking to do in a person's heart.

John 16:13 says, "The Spirit of truth ... will guide you into all truth." As we have seen, the Spirit guides us, teaches us, and convicts us—but that's just for starters. For us to obtain forgiveness, what has to happen? "If we confess our sins, He is faithful and just to forgive us our sins and to cleanse us from all unrighteousness" (1 John 1:9).

To receive God's forgiveness, we must first repent and confess. If we refuse, then we begin to head toward the point of no return. But if our hearts are, like Pharaoh's, hardened, if we see evidence of God's work in our lives but consistently and repeatedly stifle the conviction that the evidence brings, it's not likely that we are going to confess or repent of anything. How could we?

The Crucial Context

The topic of the unpardonable sin should start to be clearer now—it's like Christianity 101. We need to repent, we need to be convicted, we need to be guided, we need to know that we have done wrong, and we need to confess that wrong.

What brings about all these things in our lives? It is the work of the Holy Spirit alone. Thus, blasphemy against the Holy Spirit is rejecting and refusing to respond to the leading, the teaching, and the conviction of the Holy Spirit. It is closing the only door through which we obtain forgiveness. That's why it's the sin that cannot be forgiven.

Blasphemy against the Holy Spirit is the sin for which *we will not repent and confess;* hence, it is unpardonable, and that is why Jesus spoke so strongly about it. Let's look at the context in which Jesus uttered one of His warnings about this sin.

Matthew 12:22 reads, "Then one was brought to Him who was demon-possessed, blind and mute." This person was in bad shape: blind, unable to speak, and demon-possessed. The verse continues: "And He healed him, so that the blind and mute man both spoke and he saw." The demon was cast out, and the multitudes were amazed; they asked, "Could this be

27

the Son of David?"—in other words, "Could this be the Messiah?"

Why would they ask that? The evidence was overwhelming that Jesus had the power of God against the devil. He liberated and healed the man's sight and speech as they all stood there and watched. Imagine if you were to see a miracle like that right before your own eyes. *Someone blind suddenly being able to see; someone voiceless suddenly able to speak!*

What, though, was the reaction of the Pharisees when they heard about this miracle? "This fellow does not cast out demons except by Beelzebub, the ruler of the demons." That was a very dangerous attitude to have in the presence of God's Son: *to disregard the obvious evidence of the working of God's Spirit and to instead call it the working of the devil!*

The Pharisees called the work of Jesus the work of a pagan deity. Beelzebub was a Phoenician god, about the lowest of the low when it came to gods. Beelzebub was also known as the "Lord of the Flies," a god of filth, because when the Phoenicians saw some filth, or scum, or even a corpse, they noticed that flies would land on them and, soon, worms and maggots would appear. Not knowing about modern science, they came to the conclusion that the filth and scum of corpses somehow had the power to give life. They thought some god must have put that power in there; thus, they came to worship the "Lord of the Flies," Beelzebub. And this was the being that the religious leaders said gave Jesus His power.

Talk about pushing the envelope.

Talk about blasphemy against the Holy Spirit!

They were denying the influence and power of the Holy Spirit. That's why Jesus—knowing their thoughts—said,

> "Every kingdom divided against itself is brought to desolation, and every city or house divided against itself will not stand. If Satan casts out Satan, he is divided against himself. How then will his kingdom stand? And if I cast out demons by Beelzebub, by whom do your sons cast them out? Therefore they shall be your judges. But if I cast out demons by the Spirit of God, surely the kingdom of God has come upon you" (Matthew 12:25–28).

In other words, *"If what I'm doing is of God, then what are you men really doing and saying? What position are you taking in regard to what God is doing in this world? You are ascribing to the devil the work of the very God you claim to worship and serve."* They were refusing to acknowledge the obvious demonstration of God's Spirit. Look again at His statement in Matthew 12:28: "But if I cast out demons by the Spirit of God, surely the kingdom of God has come upon you." He was pleading with them! *"The kingdom of God is come to you. Don't reject it, don't deny it, and don't mislabel it by calling the obvious signs of that kingdom the work of the devil."*

But Jesus wasn't finished. He continued,

> "How can one enter a strong man's house and plunder his goods, unless he first binds the

strong man? And then he will plunder his house. He who is not with Me is against Me, and he who does not gather with Me scatters abroad" (Matthew 12:29, 30).

What was Jesus saying here? He was telling the Pharisees, very clearly and unambiguously, that if they weren't recognizing His work as the power of God, then they would eventually be filled with the power of the devil. There's no middle ground; we're on one side or the other. There is, indeed, a great controversy between good and evil, Christ and Satan, and we have to make our choice about whose side we are going to join in this conflict. And to be blunt: to not choose Christ is to choose the other side—the devil's side.

Now comes Jesus' zinger:

> "Therefore I say to you, every sin and blasphemy will be forgiven men, but the blasphemy against the Spirit will not be forgiven men. Anyone who speaks a word against the Son of Man, it will be forgiven him; but whoever speaks against the Holy Spirit, it will not be forgiven him, either in this age or in the age to come" (Matthew 12:31, 32).

So now we have the full context in which Jesus makes His statement about the unpardonable sin. The Pharisees refused to recognize the work of the Holy Spirit; they rejected the clear work of the Spirit of God. Don't miss this point: *If we refuse to acknowledge and recognize the working of the Holy*

Spirit in our lives, then we are at risk of committing the unpardonable sin.

Remember back in 2010, when those 33 Chilean miners were trapped 2,300 feet below the surface? A narrow, deep hole was dug through the rocky earth to rescue them. If those miners refused to heed the voice of their helpers, to escape through that tiny tunnel, they would have surely died. There was no other way for them to be saved!

Likewise, as we have seen, if the work of the Holy Spirit is to guide us into knowledge and lead us to repentance and conviction, and we reject that very work, we are in danger of committing the unpardonable sin because it's only through that work we can be brought to repentance, which ultimately leads to pardon.

One of the best definitions of the unpardonable sin that I've read comes from E. G. White. She writes,

> "No one needs look upon the sin against the Holy Ghost as something mysterious and indefinable. The sin against the Holy Ghost is the sin of persistent refusal to respond to the invitation to repent" (*That I Might Know Him*, pg. 243).

That's it … pure and simple! "The persistent refusal to repent of sin." That is the unpardonable sin.

Three Wrong Paths

Now that we better understand what the unpardonable sin is, the next question arises: How does it happen that someone gets in danger of committing it? It's fine that we know what it is, but that's only part of the issue. What's just as important is what we need to do to make sure we don't commit it!

What happens, then, that causes people to commit the unpardonable sin—to place themselves in a position where they can't be saved, where they have crossed the point of no return? It happens like this …

Almost imperceptibly, the conscience is seared and the heart is hardened. In fact, this is why it is counted as such a terrible sin. Sometimes people don't understand why God considers this the worst thing that can be done, but it is because the Holy Spirit is the only way God can reach an individual with the message of salvation. That is the way we are led to repentance. If we did not have the Holy Spirit, there would be no hope for us, because we have to repent in order to be forgiven. If we have no sense of our need of repentance, we won't do it and, therefore, we won't be forgiven.

Again, it's like a deep-sea diver. His oxygen tank has the air he needs to live. His dive computer is always working to let him know when he's in danger of running out of air. But if he ignores the computer and continues to descend when he knows he should start ascending, he's going to run out of air and drown. If he obeys the warnings of his dive computer and makes his way to the surface, he will live. But he has no way of knowing that it's getting dangerous for him but by his dive computer—so is it wise for him to ignore it? In the same way, in this sin-darkened world, the only way God can reach us is through the Holy Spirit.

In our analogy, God is the air we need to live; Jesus is the salvation at the surface. The Holy Spirit is the dive computer—He warns us that our spiritual tank is running out of God and we need to surface to Jesus to be saved. But if we turn away from the Spirit, if we refuse to listen and obey our spiritual dive computer, God will have to let us go; thus, we will be lost. And it was our choice!

This was why King David was so deeply concerned in his great prayer of contrition. While pouring out his heart to God in Psalm 51, David prayed, "Do not cast me away from Your presence, and do not take Your Holy Spirit from me" (verse 11). He realized that if God removed the Holy Spirit from his life, he was lost. He would be left alone with no way of being saved. That's why Jesus said this sin is the unpardonable sin. When you cut yourself off and refuse to listen to the Holy Spirit, there is no hope for you.

Now, there are three specific ways in which people can commit this hopeless sin.

---

1) The first way is for a person to simply admit in his life, "I don't want to be saved; I don't want to be bothered with God and the Bible." Once in a while, you'll find a person like this—but not too often. Most people really want to be saved, but now and then you'll find someone who just isn't interested at all. He's satisfied with his materialistic world even though he knows it will ultimately lead to a complete dead end for him.

Proverbs 28:13 says: "He who covers his sins will not prosper, but whoever confesses and forsakes them will have mercy." Those who don't want to give up their sins will finally convince themselves that they are happy without Christ. While God is extremely patient with a person, the time will eventually come when someone feels no conviction and the Holy Spirit will leave them alone. God is not in the business of forcing anyone to follow Him. We simply have to leave someone like this in God's hands, for He alone is Judge. Only God knows their hearts and how much sand is left in the hourglass.

2) **The second way,** which is so vulnerable to this sin, reaches the same state of rejection but by a different route. The person on this path truly feels he wants to be saved and will tell everyone that it is his desire to get right with God. Unfortunately, this person keeps waiting—and only waiting—for a better moment to step onto the path of total surrender. He allows those golden moments with the Holy Spirit to slip by until his will has been paralyzed by indecision.

Such a person still talks about following Christ, but his ability to act is ultimately paralyzed by procrastination. He dawdles, obfuscates, and makes a lot of excuses for sins he's unwilling to let go, but he never makes the genuine surrender he needs to. Finally, he lingers too long, slowly passing by the PNR. He just keeps going through the motions of good intentions, utterly self-deceived in regard to his true condition, until the engine sputters and he ditches into the sea of outer darkness.

3) Without a doubt, the largest group of unpardonable sinners can be found on a **third pathway.**

What's strange, however, is that a person in this group appears to be the most unlikely person ever to commit the unpardonable sin. He is a church member—perhaps even a pillar in the congregation. Why then, is he in great danger—perhaps even worse danger than those on the previous pathways we mentioned? Because he does not understand that truth is progressive.

Millions of Christians have settled back in their comfortable pews, complacent about their salvation. They feel secure in their conformity to a church, not realizing that baptism is only the beginning of a long, growing experience. Said the psalmist: "Your word is a lamp to my feet and a light to my path" (Psalm 119:105). The further we walk into the Bible, the more truth is revealed and the more accountable we become before God. He has never unfolded all the truth to any one person at any one time. A lamp only shines far enough to expose one safe step. As we step into that space, another space is revealed. As we grow in grace and knowledge, God requires us to move with the advancing light of truth. When we don't—when we think God asks too much of us—we step back, refusing to go forward. For many, the next step is backward...and back again...until the Holy Spirit's influence is totally ignored.

In a real sense, then, especially with this last group, everything depends on what we do with the truths God has already given to us. James wrote, "To him who knows to do good and does not do it, to him it is sin" (4:17). It doesn't really matter an iota whether we are rich or poor or identify ourselves as Catholic or Jew or Protestant; the big issue is whether we are acting upon what we know.

Jesus expands on this crucial principle in John chapter 15, again in the context of those who had every reason to believe in Him yet refused to act upon those reasons. "If I had not come and spoken to them, they would have no sin, but now they have no excuse for their sin" (verse 22). In other words, they didn't have any excuse for their rejection of Jesus; it was, instead, the hardness of their hearts that closed their minds to the conviction of truth.

Accountability

Who, then, is accountable and chargeable before God? Those who have been enlightened, in whatever degree, by the Holy Spirit through the Word.

The sincere soul who seeks to be faithful to all she knows, be it much or little, will be accepted. Sin will be counted only against those who have heard truth, one way or another, and have rejected it by choosing to be their own gods, by making their own rules, by following the dictates of their own hardened consciences—instead of following the clear commands and admonitions of God.

In the same vein, Christ warned these people, "If you were blind, you would have no sin; but now you say, 'We see.' Therefore your sin remains" (John 9:41). The whole problem of the unpardonable sin revolves around the issue of obeying what we know to be true. On another occasion, Jesus said, "Walk while you have the light, lest darkness overtake you" (John 12:35). And from where does this light come? The Holy

Spirit, who guides us into all truth. When we refuse to obey what we know to be the truth, we are rejecting the ministry of the Spirit. We literally drive away the Person whom God has sent to light our way, admitting that we'd rather live in darkness.

Can you see just how self-destructive this hardness of our hearts can be? God's special messenger is grieved away by our deliberate refusal to respond to His invitations of mercy. As we saw before, God said long ago that His Spirit will not always strive with man. At one point He'll say to the Holy Spirit, *"Let them alone. If they insist having their own way, do not pursue them any longer."*

We see a prime example of this in the book of Hosea, when the Lord says, "Ephraim is joined to idols, let him alone. Their drink is rebellion, they commit harlotry *continually.* Her rulers dearly love dishonor" (Hosea 4:17, 18, emphasis added). Notice, the problem wasn't just their "harlotry," an expression that symbolizes spiritual unfaithfulness, usually by following after pagan religious practices. It's the fact that they did this "continually," to the point where the Lord said to basically not bother trying to turn them around.

In fact, their leaders *loved* "dishonor." They had reached the point of no return.

A Seared Conscience

How do people get caught up in these deadly spiritual traps? The apostle Paul wrote: "Now the Spirit expressly says that in latter times some will depart from the faith, giving heed to deceiving spirits and doctrines of demons, speaking lies in hypocrisy, having their own *conscience seared* with a hot iron" (1 Timothy 4:1, 2, emphasis added).

Who speaks? It's the Holy Spirit. But if you don't listen, then you won't hear it. The key word in this text, for our purposes, is "seared"; it actually sounds in Greek like the English word "cauterized."

During the Civil War, when a soldier received a serious wound on the battlefield, and it was bleeding and doctors had no other way to stop it, they would actually heat up a sword in a fire until it was red hot. They would then lay it on the wound, cauterizing it to help stop the bleeding.

Of course, that's not the preferred way to do it today. It was, though, a battlefield emergency procedure. The problem, however, was that the practice also killed some of the nerve endings; as a result, the wounded soldier would often lose some feeling in that area of the body.

We briefly covered this idea already, but it is worth repeating: If your nerves are damaged, deadened, and not working, then they won't let you know when your body is in danger. You can get hurt worse than you otherwise would because there isn't any pain to warn you about the danger.

Now, it's bad enough when this deadening happens to your body. But what about when it happens to your conscience? That's what Paul was warning about in his letter to Timothy. A person can sear, or cauterize, his conscience until he is so used to committing a certain sin that he can actually get to the point where he is no longer the least bit bothered by it—he feels no more guilt—just like the proverbial boiling frog, who sits calmly in a pot of water as it slowly heats up until it boils the pathetic creature alive.

Let's suppose you see the light from the lamp of God's Word but refuse to obey it. The Holy Spirit has convicted you, and you understand perfectly what God requires, but it is unpopular and especially inconvenient to your lifestyle. What happens if you persist in disregarding that light and reject the truth the Spirit has revealed for any reason whatsoever?

The Spirit will continue to speak to you, of course, and for a time the battle in your conscience will still be waged. You will feel miserable and guilty. Days will pass by, and even months, while you keep on violating the conviction of what is right. Gradually, however, your conscience will begin to adjust to what is being done by your body. Slowly the feelings of guilt will begin to subside; the acts of disobedience will become less and less objectionable to your conscience. In fact, at some point along the way, you won't feel anything at all regarding what you once felt terrible about doing! Your conscience will have been seared; your spiritual nerves will have been cut apart.

Finally, the truth that seemed so clear and uncomplicated in the beginning will turn into a muddle of uncertainty. Rationalizations will spring forth to justify your disobedience, and the early convictions of sin will fade away. Life will be almost as comfortable as it was before the light came.

What happened to you? You persistently sinned against the Holy Spirit and now you are sinking into the numb state of indifference and drifting toward the unpardonable sin.

The Alarm Clock With a Snooze Button

A mobster once confessed about the first time he killed a man. He had felt terrible. The next time he took a life? He admitted he felt pretty bad—but not as bad as the first time. But each time he ended a life in violence, it bothered him less and less until it actually got to the point that it didn't bother him anymore and he started to like it!

It's like that person who lives by the airport. When you visit him, you hear the jets roar over the end of the runway and you think, "How in the world does he endure living here?" Everything in his home is shaking on the shelves, but it doesn't seem like he even notices it. He just gets used to it.

It's hard for us to imagine it, but that's really the way it is with sin if we're not careful. From the book *Amazing Grace,* page 215:

> "Whatever the sin, if the soul repents and believes, the guilt is washed away in the blood of Christ; but he who rejects the work of the Holy Spirit is placing himself where repentance and faith cannot come to him. It is by the Spirit of God and His work upon the heart that men are saved. When men willfully reject the Spirit, and declare it to be from Satan, they cut off the channel by which God communicates with them. When the Spirit is finally rejected, there is no more that God can do for the soul" (E. G. White).

The unpardonable sin is never forgiven because it is never confessed and repented of. Look at this Scripture again: "If we confess our sins, He is faithful and just to forgive us our sins and to cleanse us from all unrighteousness" (1 John 1:9). Notice, what is the condition for having our sins forgiven and being cleansed from unrighteousness? We have to confess and repent. If we don't feel the need of doing that—we won't! And without confession and repentance, there is no salvation.

Now, this is a crucial point: *The unpardonable sin isn't really one particular act that can be isolated and labeled.* It can be any sin, no matter how "small," which is cherished in the face of light and truth. It actually is a condition of seared sensitivity that is brought on by persistent disobedience to known truth. It isn't something that happens one time; rather, it's over a period of time, little by little, refusing to repent. It's toying with and gambling with God's mercy.

For example, think about those alarm clocks in hotels. They come in handy when you are way out of your normal time zone, you have to get up early, and you happen to be very tired. The alarm goes off and you think, "*Oh, man, just five more minutes.*" And so you hit the snooze button, roll over, and fall back to sleep. And then the alarm goes off again. "*Oh, man, just five more minutes.*" At some point, you might actually heed the alarm and get up. But over time, if you keep pushing the snooze button and rolling over to get back to sleep, you'll get to a point where you're so used to hitting the snooze button that you just sleep through the whole process. You can even "program" your subconscious to not even hear the alarm anymore. You don't even need to reach for the snooze button.

The analogy is obvious: We can persistently ignore the promptings of the Holy Spirit, hitting the spiritual snooze button and so searing our conscience by continued wrongdoing that we get completely hardened to God's promptings. Don't miss that word "continued." We are not talking about the sporadic wrong act or sin, which we all have done. Instead, we're talking about a relationship—a walk—a day-by-day, week-by-week, year-by-year choice on our part to stay connected to God by obeying His Word. In the book *Steps to Christ,* E. G. White again clarifies, "It's not the occasional misdeed or the occasional good deed that determines whose side we're on. It's the habitual words and acts."

You can very much tell where a person's heart is by his habitual words and acts. What is the trend of his life? Which direction is he going? Though it's important to be very careful about making judgments about others, we need to be adamant about making them about ourselves. We are made up of choices in life; what do your choices say about your walk with Christ and the kind of life you are living? No wonder Paul wrote: "Examine yourselves as to whether you are in the faith. Test yourselves. Do you not know yourselves, that Jesus Christ is in you?—unless indeed you are disqualified" (2 Corinthians 13:5).

Yes, we all have done wrong and, chances are, we will slip again in the future. But that's not the same as persistently indulging in things that we know to be wrong but justify to ourselves nonetheless. "*Oh, it's not so bad. That other guy in church does much worse things."* Or … *"I'll stop eventually—but not now, not today."* Or … *"Who am I really hurting by this sin?"* Or … *"Well, everyone else does it, so how bad can it really be?"*

If these thoughts sound familiar, take heed. Don't be like the man on the beach who went too far and couldn't make it back. Heed the warning signs before it's too late!

The Time to Repent Is Now

Suppose, as you've read this book, you've recognized this pattern within yourself. You're worried you've done some of these very things. What can you do?

The key is to repent *now*. Not tomorrow … not next Thursday … not after the next office party. The time is now, because tomorrow, or next Thursday, or after the office party, you might no longer sense the need to repent. Every delay you succumb to will callous your conscience just a little bit more. Human hearts are so easily deceived that we really don't know just how hard and deadened our spiritual nerves already might be.

Repentance is a gift of the Holy Spirit. If we are hardened to the Spirit, we will not repent when given the chance. And without that repentance, without sorrow for sin, there is no salvation. Few things are more tragic than someone who has been raised in a Christian environment, who knows and believes the truth, but thinks: *"I'll repent at the end of my life right before I die. I'm going to live for myself and the world, but God is so gracious I'm going to wait until the eleventh hour to repent and be saved."*

People will point to the story of the thief on the cross, who offered up a last-minute repentance and was given assurance of his salvation. A thief! As he hung on the cross next to Jesus, he said, "Lord, remember me when You come into Your kingdom," and Jesus answered, "You will be with Me in Paradise" (Luke 23:42, 43). From that story, the thinking goes: *"After all, he repented! All he said was 'Lord, remember me.' That was all it took for him to be saved, so that's just what I'll do at the end of the road. I've got it figured out—I'll get all the pleasure of sin and then I'll give the leftovers to God just before I die."*

There is, indeed, great encouragement for us in the story of the thief; however, it's important not to read more into the story than is warranted. We don't know how distant he was from God. But we do know that upon seeing Jesus and being convicted of who Jesus was, *he instantly repented.* At the moment of conviction, he acted.

It's a world of difference—the experience of the thief and someone who, perhaps even a Christian, purposely rejects the promptings of the Spirit and rationalizes that rejection for many years by thinking that, like the thief on the cross, he can just turn it around at the end. This is tragically dangerous! The conscience will likely be long dead to the Spirit after 70 years of presumptuous sin. Besides, not everyone knows when they'll die and, thus, have the time to repent! How many people wake one morning thinking it's just another day … but by dinnertime are dead?

We can be sure of this: The story of the thief on the cross was not meant to teach us that a person can safely delay surrendering to the Lord when prompted to repent by the Holy Spirit. Such delays, if persisted in, will lead to the unpardonable sin. Mathew Henry wrote, "There is one death bed repentance recorded in the Bible so that no one despair, but there is *only* one, so that no one will presume."

Have I Committed the Unpardonable Sin?

All that we have studied so far leads us to this final question: *How can a person know if he or she has committed the unpardonable sin?*

It's not uncommon at Amazing Facts to hear from people who fear they might have driven away the Holy Spirit once and for all. The ministry frequently gets emails and calls from people who are terrified they have committed the unpardonable sin. Many of these people think they have reached the point of no return because of the terrible things they have done in their lives. They are worried and desperate for an answer.

I believe we can give them clear, positive assurance that they are not guilty of this sin. If so, they likely wouldn't be concerned about the things of God. Certainly they would not be watching our programs, coming to our prophecy seminars, searching our websites, taking our Bible Studies, *or even choosing to read this book* unless the Holy Spirit were still drawing them and creating a desire in them for truth and salvation.

In other words, the mere fact that they are concerned about their spiritual state, the mere fact that they are asking this question, is encouraging evidence they have not reached the PNR. No one has grieved away the Holy Spirit if they still have a conviction of sin and a drawing to God. Those who search and seek after spiritual truth have not committed the unpardonable sin.

Here's a true story about a "mountain man" named John Johnson. At one time he had to cross 100 miles of snow-covered plains in the middle of winter around Yosemite because hostiles were pursuing him. One night in the bitter cold, he dug straight down into the snow to make a shelter from the freezing winds. At one point, he noticed that, while drifting off to sleep, he was overwhelmed with a sense of warmth and comfort. Amid all this biting cold, he felt a strange warm glow. It might seem like a blessing, but Johnson, exhausted as he was, knew what it really meant: This sensation was an early sign of hypothermia. The cold had so numbed his body that he no longer felt the cold. He was being anesthetized into a sleep of death. He wanted so much just to give up, give in, and go to sleep. It felt so good. But he knew that if he gave in, he would never wake again. So he forced himself to crawl out of the hole and expose himself, again, to that miserable weather just to stay alive. He continued his plod and made it to safety.

You see, the most deceptive aspect of the unpardonable sin is people's illusion of comfort in living without God. Their lives are finally "free" from the conflicting turmoil of struggling with conscience. It didn't happen overnight—the nagging convictions grew fainter and fainter, blending at last into a contented, satisfied lifestyle. If you're experiencing discomfort in your sin, then the Holy Spirit is probably still working in your life.

Christians shouldn't marvel at the display of an unconverted soul's "peace of mind." That deadly malaise is apparent only in those who no longer have two voices, two natures, contending for mastery. Job describes this temporary illusion of peace:

> "Why do the wicked live and become old, yes, become mighty in power? Their descendants are established with them in their sight, and their offspring before their eyes.... They sing to the tambourine and harp, and rejoice to the sound of the flute. They spend their days in wealth, and in a moment go down to the grave. Yet they say to God, 'Depart from us, for we do not desire the knowledge of Your ways'" (Job 21:7–14).

With the Holy Spirit out of the picture, the flesh enjoys uncontested control over the heart and life. No more spiritual battles rage, and the unpardonable sin even appears to have brought a measure of relief. Like a penned turkey being fattened before Thanksgiving, the unconverted think life is so good. But that mirage covers an empty soul hardened in sin and heading down a path to sure destruction.

The Scripture describes the Lord as "merciful and gracious, longsuffering, and abounding in goodness and truth, keeping mercy for thousands, forgiving iniquity and transgression and sin, by no means clear-ing the guilty" (Exodus 34:6, 7).

Yes, there is a limit to God's mercy, but most people who fear committing the unpardonable sin have not because they have underestimated God's patience and mercy. Remember, Jesus prayed for the forgiveness of those who crucified Him! He gave the apostle Paul forgiveness even though he had killed Christ's followers!

A state elementary teacher received a phone call and was asked to visit a child in a large city hospital. She took the boy's name and room number and was told by the teacher on the other end of the line, "We're studying nouns and adverbs in his class now. I'd be grateful if you could help him with his homework so he doesn't fall behind the others." It wasn't until the visiting teacher got outside the boy's room that she re-alized it was located in the hospital's burn unit.

No one had prepared her to find this ten-year-old boy so horribly burned and in such great pain. After she entered the room, once he saw her, she felt that she couldn't just turn and walk out, so she awkwardly stammered, "I'm the hospital teacher, and your teach-er sent me to help you with nouns and adverbs." She stumbled through her lesson and then excused herself. The next morning a nurse on the burn unit asked her, "What did you do to that boy?" Before she could fin-ish a profusion of apologies, the nurse interrupted her: "You don't understand. We've been very worried about him, but ever since you were here yesterday, his whole attitude has changed. He's fighting back, responding to treatment—it's as though he's suddenly decided to live."

The boy later explained that he had completely given up hope until he saw that teacher. It all changed when he came to a simple realization. With joyful tears he expressed it this way: "They wouldn't send a teacher to work on nouns and adverbs with a dying boy, would they?" When he realized he still had homework, he knew there was still hope.

In short, those who fear they have committed the unpardonable sin generally haven't; that fear demonstrates that the Spirit is pleading with them, teaching them and bringing conviction into their hearts. Of course, that's a good sign—but it's not enough. The crucial question remaining for them now is: "The Holy Spirit is calling you to complete surrender to the Lord in faith, love, and obedience: Will you obey?"

If you sense that calling, don't delay; follow it *immediately* with all your heart—and do it *today*. Ask Him *now* to save you. God would not have sent His Son to suffer and die to save you unless it was possible for you to be saved. This message is the message of the Holy Spirit working in your life.

"Today, if you will hear His voice, do not harden your hearts" … or by this time tomorrow you could have crossed over the point of no return.

The UNPARDONABLE Sin • A Bible Study

To help you retain, ingrain, and apply the information you've just learned in this booklet, we have included a short Bible study on the subject of salvation and the unpardonable sin in an easy-to-understand, question-and-answer format. Thank you to Amazing Facts for the study. (Bible passages taken from the King James Version unless otherwise noted.)

1. What is the sin that God cannot forgive?

"All manner of sin and blasphemy shall be forgiven unto men: but the blasphemy against the Holy Ghost shall not be forgiven unto men" (Matthew 12:31).

Answer: The sin God cannot forgive is "blasphemy against the Holy Ghost." Christians have many differing beliefs about this sin. Some believe it is murder; some, cursing the Holy Ghost; some, committing suicide; some, killing an unborn child; some, denial of Christ; some, a heinous, horrible, extremely wicked act; and others, worshipping a false god. The next question will shed some helpful light on this crucial matter. (By the way, the word "ghost" comes from "ghast," the Old English word for "spirit.")

2. What does the Bible say about sin and blasphemy?

"All manner of sin and blasphemy shall be forgiven unto men" (Matthew 12:31).

Answer: The Bible clearly states that all kinds of sin and blasphemy will be forgiven. So none of the sins listed in the previous answer is the sin that God cannot forgive. In fact, no single act of any kind is the unpardonable sin!

> **Sounds Contradictory:** Yes, it sounds contradictory, but both of the following statements are true:
>
> **A.** Any and every kind of sin and blasphemy will be forgiven.
>
> **B.** The blasphemy or sin against the Holy Spirit will not be forgiven.
>
> **Jesus Made Both Statements:** Jesus made both statements in Matthew 12:31, so there is no error. To harmonize these statements, we must learn about the work of the Holy Ghost.

3. **What is the work of the Holy Spirit?**

> *"He [the Holy Spirit] will convict the world of sin, and of righteousness, and of judgment. ... He will guide you into all truth" (John 16:8, 13 NKJV).*

Answer: The work of the Holy Spirit is to convict you of sin and to guide you into all truth. The Holy Spirit is God's agency for conversion. Without the Holy Spirit, no one feels sorrow for sin, nor is anyone ever converted.

4. **When the Holy Spirit convinces you of sin, what must you do to be forgiven?**

"If we confess our sins, he is faithful and just to forgive us our sins, and to cleanse us from all unrighteousness" (1 John 1:9).

Answer: When convicted of sin by the Holy Spirit, you must confess your sins in order to be forgiven. When you confess them, God not only forgives you but He also miraculously cleanses you from all unrighteousness. God is waiting and ready to forgive you for any and every sin you might commit (Psalm 86:5), but *only if* you confess and forsake it.

5. **What happens if you do not confess your sins when convicted by the Holy Spirit?**

"He that covereth his sins shall not prosper: but whoso confesseth and forsaketh them shall have mercy" (Proverbs 28:13).

Answer: If you do not confess your sins, Jesus cannot forgive your sins. Thus, any sin that you do not confess is unpardonable until you confess it, because forgiveness always follows confession. It never precedes it.

Danger of Resisting the Holy Spirit: Resisting the Holy Spirit is terribly dangerous because it so easily leads to rejection of the Holy Spirit, which is the sin God can never forgive. It is passing the point of no return. Since the Holy Spirit is the only agency given to bring you conviction, if you permanently reject Him, your case is thereafter hopeless. This subject is so important that God illustrates and explains it many different ways in Scripture. Watch for these different explanations as you continue exploring this Bible study.

6. **When the Holy Spirit convicts you of sin or leads you to new truth, when should you act?**

Answer: The Bible says:

   A. *"As soon as they hear of me, they shall obey me" (Psalm 18:44).*

   B. *"I made haste, and delayed not to keep thy commandments" (Psalm 119:60).*

   C. *"Now is the accepted time; behold, now is the day of salvation" (2 Corinthians 6:2).*

   D. *"Now why tarriest thou? arise, and be baptised, and wash away thy sins, calling on the name of the Lord" (Acts 22:16).*

The Bible repeatedly states that when you are convicted of sin, you must confess it at once. And when you learn new truth, you must accept it without delay.

7. **What solemn warning does God give about the pleading of His Holy Spirit?**

   "My spirit shall not always strive with man" (Genesis 6:3).

Answer: God solemnly warns that the Holy Spirit does not indefinitely continue pleading with a person to turn from sin and obey God.

8. **At what point does the Holy Spirit stop pleading with a person?**

   "Therefore speak I to them in parables: because… hearing they hear not" (Matthew 13:13).

Answer: The Holy Spirit stops talking to a person when that individual becomes deaf to His voice. The Bible describes it as hearing, but hearing not. There is no point in setting the alarm on a clock in the room of a person who cannot hear. Likewise, a person can condition himself to not hear an alarm clock ring by repeatedly shutting it off and not getting up. The day finally comes when the alarm goes off and he does not hear it.

Don't Shut Off the Holy Spirit: So it is with the Holy Spirit. If you keep shutting Him off, one day He will speak to you and you will not hear Him. When that day comes, the Spirit sadly turns away from you because you have become deaf to His pleadings. What a solemn warning against resisting the Spirit's voice!

9. **What does Ephesians 4:30 have to say about the Holy Spirit?**

Answer: The verse says, "Grieve not the holy Spirit of God, whereby ye are sealed unto the day of redemption." Paul implies here that the Holy Spirit can be grieved away by our rejection of His loving appeals. As a courtship can be ended forever by the repeated refusal of one party to the other's wooing, so our relationship with the Holy Spirit can end permanently by our persistent refusal to respond to His loving appeals.

10. **God, through His Holy Spirit, brings light (John 1:9) and conviction (John 16:8) to every person. What must you do when you receive light from the Holy Spirit?**

"The path of the just is as the shining light, that shineth more and more unto the perfect day. The way of the wicked is as darkness" (Proverbs 4:18, 19). "Walk while ye have the light, lest darkness come upon you" (John 12:35).

Answer: The Bible rule is that when the Holy Spirit brings you new light or conviction of sin, you must act at once—obey without delay. If you obey and walk in the light as you receive it, God will continue giving you light. If you refuse, even the light that you have will go out and you will be left in darkness. The darkness that comes from a persistent and final refusal to follow light is the result of rejecting the Spirit, and it leaves you without hope.

11. In the parable of the sower (Luke 8:5–18), what is meant by the seed that fell by the wayside and was eaten by birds?

Answer: The Bible says, "The seed is the word of God. Those by the way side are they that hear; then cometh the devil, and taketh away the word out of their hearts, lest they should believe and be saved" (Luke 8:11, 12). Jesus is pointing out that when we understand what the Holy Spirit is asking us to do regarding some new light from the Scripture, we must act at once. Otherwise, the devil has the opportunity to remove that truth from our minds.

12. Can any sin become a sin against the Holy Spirit?

Answer: Yes! If you steadfastly refuse to confess and forsake any sin, you will eventually become deaf to the Holy Spirit's pleading. The following are some Bible examples:

A. Judas' unpardonable sin was covetousness (John 12:6). Was it because God could not forgive it? No! It became unpardonable only because Judas refused to listen to the Holy Spirit and confess his sin. Eventually he became deaf to the Spirit's voice.

B. Lucifer's unpardonable sins were pride and self-exaltation (Isaiah 14:12–14). Lucifer could have been pardoned and cleansed from these sins, but he refused to listen until he could no longer hear the Spirit's voice.

C. The Pharisees' unpardonable sin was refusal to accept Jesus as the Messiah (Mark 3:22–30). They were convinced repeatedly with deep, heartfelt conviction that Jesus was the Son of the living God. But they hardened their hearts and stubbornly refused to accept Him as their Savior and Lord. Finally they grew deaf to the Spirit's voice. Then one day, after another miracle by Jesus, the Pharisees told the multitude that Jesus received His power from the devil. Christ at once told them that attributing His power to the devil indicated they had passed the point of no return and blasphemed the Holy Ghost. God could have, and joyfully would have, forgiven them. But they refused the Holy Spirit's voice and could no longer be reached.

You Cannot Choose the Consequences: When the Spirit makes His appeal, you can choose to respond or refuse, but you cannot choose the consequences. They are fixed. If you consistently respond, you will become more like Jesus and be assured of a place in God's heavenly kingdom. If you persistently refuse, you will grieve the Holy Spirit away and He will leave you forever, sealing your doom.

13. After King David had committed the sins of adultery and murder, what anguished prayer did he pray?

"Take not thy holy spirit from me" (Psalm 51:11).

Answer: He pleaded with God not to take the Holy Spirit away from him. Why? Because David knew if the Holy Spirit left him, he was doomed from that moment. He knew that only the Holy Spirit could lead him to repentance and restoration, and he trembled at the thought of becoming deaf to His voice. The Bible tells us in another place that God finally left Ephraim alone because he was joined to his idols (Hosea 4:17) and would not listen to the Spirit. He had become spiritually deaf. The most tragic thing that can happen to any person is for God to turn away and leave him alone. Don't let it happen to you!

14. What crucial command did Paul give to the church in Thessalonica?

"Quench not the Spirit" (1 Thessalonians 5:19).

Answer: The Holy Spirit's pleading is like a fire that burns in a person's mind and heart. Sin has the same effect on the Holy Spirit as water has on fire. As you ignore the Holy Spirit and continue in sin, you pour water on the fire of the Holy Spirit. Don't quench the fire of the Holy Spirit by repeatedly refusing to heed the Spirit's voice. If the fire goes out, you'll pass the point of no return.

Any Sin Can Quench the Fire: Any unconfessed or unforsaken sin can ultimately snuff out the fire of the Holy Spirit. It could be refusal to keep God's holy Sabbath. It could be failure to forgive one who has betrayed or otherwise injured you. It could be immorality. Refusal to obey the Holy Spirit's voice in any area pours water on the fire of the Holy Spirit. Don't put out the fire.

15. What other shocking statement did Paul make to the Thessalonian church?

"And with all deceivableness of unrighteousness in them that perish; because they received not the love of the truth, that they might be saved. And for this cause God shall send them strong delusion, that they should believe a lie: That they all might be damned [lost] who believed not the truth, but had pleasure in unrighteousness" (2 Thessalonians 2:10–12).

Answer: What sobering words! God says that those who refuse to receive the truth and conviction brought by the Holy Spirit will (after the Spirit departs from them) receive a strong delusion to believe that error is truth.

16. What wrenching experience will those who have been sent these strong delusions face on judgment day?

"Many will say to me in that day, Lord, Lord, have we not prophesied in thy name? and in thy name have cast out devils? and in thy name done many

wonderful works? And then will I profess unto them, I never knew you: depart from me, ye that work iniquity" (Matthew 7:22, 23).

Answer: Those who are crying "Lord, Lord" will be shocked that they are shut out. They will be absolutely positive they are saved. Jesus will then doubtless remind them of that crucial time in their lives when the Holy Spirit brought new truth and conviction. It was clear and obviously true. It kept them awake nights, troubled and wrestling over a decision. How their hearts burned within them! Finally, they said, "No!" And they refused to listen further to the Holy Spirit. Then came a strong delusion that caused them to feel saved when they were lost.

17. **What words of warning does Jesus give to help people avoid believing they are saved when they might be lost?**

"Not every one that saith unto me, Lord, Lord, shall enter into the kingdom of heaven; but he that doeth the will of my Father which is in heaven" (Matthew 7:21).

Answer: Jesus warned that not all who have the feeling of assurance will enter His kingdom, but rather, only those who do His will. All of us desire assurance of salvation, but there is a false offer of assurance sweeping churches today that promises people salvation while people continue living in sin and manifest no changed lifestyle whatsoever.

Jesus Clears the Air: Jesus says that true assurance is only for those who do His Father's will. When you accept Jesus as Lord, your lifestyle will change radically. You will become a new creature (2 Corinthians 5:17). You will gladly keep His commandments (John 14:15) and joyously follow where He leads (1 Peter 2:21). His resurrection power (Philippians 3:10) transforms you into His image (2 Corinthians 3:18). His glorious peace floods your life (John 14:27). With Jesus dwelling in you through His Spirit (Ephesians 3:16, 17), you "can do all things" (Philippians 4:13) and "nothing shall be impossible" (Matthew 17:20).

True Assurance Versus Counterfeit Assurance: As you follow where Jesus leads, He promises that no one can take you out of His hand (John 10:28) and that a crown of life awaits you (Revelation 2:10). What amazing, genuine security Jesus has given you! Assurance promised under any other conditions is counterfeit. It will lead people to feel certain they are saved when they are, in fact, lost (Proverbs 16:25).

18. What is God's promise to you if you crown Him Lord of your life?

"He which hath begun a good work in you will perform it until the day of Jesus Christ" (Philippians 1:6). "For it is God which worketh in you both to will and to do of his good pleasure" (Philippians 2:13).

Answer: If you make Jesus the Lord of your life, He promises you miracles that will see you safely through to His eternal kingdom. Nothing could be better!

19. What additional glorious promise does Jesus make to us all?

"Behold, I stand at the door, and knock: if any man hear my voice, and open the door, I will come in to him, and will sup with him, and he with me" (Revelation 3:20).

Answer: Jesus promises to enter our lives when we open the door to Him. It is Jesus who knocks on the door of your heart through His Holy Spirit. He—the King of kings, the Savior of the world—takes time to come to you for friendly, caring guidance. What folly that we should ever be too busy or too disinterested to form a warm, loving, lasting friendship with Jesus. Jesus' friends will be in no danger of being rejected on judgment day. Jesus will personally welcome them into His kingdom (Matthew 25:34).

20. I'm deeply concerned that I may have rejected the Holy Spirit and cannot be forgiven. Do I have any hope?

Answer: You have not rejected the Holy Spirit! You can know that because you feel concerned or convicted. It is only the Holy Spirit who brings you concern and conviction (John 16:8–13). If the Holy Spirit had left you, there would be no concern or conviction in your heart. Rejoice and praise God! Give Him your life now! And prayerfully follow and obey Him in the days ahead. He will give you victory (1 Corinthians 15:57), uphold you (Philippians 2:13), and keep you until His second coming (Philippians 1:6).

"... the one who comes to Me I will by no means cast out" (John 6:37 NKJV).